EVERGREEN PARK PUBLIC LIBRARY

3 2778 00139 9651

W9-BRJ-544

1/09

EVERGREEN PARK PUBLIC LIBRARY
9400 S. TROY AVENUE
EVERGREEN PARK, IL 60805

DEMCO

Native Americans

Yokut

EVERGREEN PARK PUBLIC LIBRARY
9400 S. TROY AVENUE
EVERGREEN PARK, IL 60805

Barbara A. Gray-Kanatiiosh

ABDO Publishing Company

visit us at
www.abdopub.com

Published by ABDO Publishing Company, 4940 Viking Drive, Suite 622, Edina, Minnesota 55435. Copyright © 2004 by Abdo Consulting Group, Inc. International copyrights reserved in all countries. No part of this book may be reproduced in any form without written permission from the publisher.

Printed in the United States.

Cover Photo: Corbis
Interior Photos: Corbis pp. 4, 28, 29, 30
Illustrations: David Kanietakeron Fadden pp. 7, 9, 11, 13, 15, 17, 19, 21, 23, 25, 27
Editors: Kate A. Conley, Jennifer R. Krueger, Kristin Van Cleaf
Art Direction & Maps: Neil Klinepier

Library of Congress Cataloging-in-Publication Data

Gray-Kanatiiosh, Barbara A., 1963-
   Yokut / Barbara A. Gray-Kanatiiosh.
     p. cm. -- (Native Americans)
   Summary: An introduction to the history, social life and customs, and present life of the Yokut Indians, a tribe in California.
   Includes bibliographical references and index.
   ISBN 1-57765-942-2
   1. Yokuts Indians--Juvenile literature. [1.Yokuts Indians. 2. Indians of North America--California.] I. Title. II. Native Americans (Edina, Minn.)

   E99.Y75G72 2003
   979.4004'9741--dc21

                                                    2003045396

About the Author: Barbara A. Gray-Kanatiiosh, JD

Barbara Gray-Kanatiiosh, JD, Ph.D. ABD, is an Akwesasne Mohawk. She resides at the Mohawk Nation and is of the Wolf Clan. She has a Juris Doctorate from Arizona State University, where she was one of the first recipients of ASU's special certificate in Indian Law. Barbara's Ph.D. is in Justice Studies at ASU. She is currently working on her dissertation, which concerns the impacts of environmental injustice on indigenous culture. Barbara works hard to educate children about Native Americans through her writing and Web site, where children may ask questions and receive a written response about the Haudenosaunee culture. The Web site is: www.peace4turtleisland.org

About the Illustrator: David Kanietakeron Fadden

David Kanietakeron Fadden is a member of the Akwesasne Mohawk Wolf Clan. His work has appeared in publications such as *Akwesasne Notes*, *Indian Time*, and the *Northeast Indian Quarterly*. Examples of his work have also appeared in various publications of the Six Nations Indian Museum in Onchiota, NY. His work has also appeared in "How the West Was Lost: Always the Enemy," produced by Gannett Production, which appeared on the Discovery Channel. David's work has been exhibited in Albany, NY; the Lake Placid Center for the Arts; Centre Strathearn in Montreal, Quebec; North Country Community College in Saranac Lake, NY; Paul Smith's College in Paul Smiths, NY; and at the Unison Arts & Learning Center in New Paltz, NY.

Contents

Where They Lived

The Yokut (YOHK-oc) were a group of about 50 separate tribes. Each tribe spoke a different dialect from the Penutian language family. Their neighbors included the Miwok, Salinan, and Chumash peoples.

The Yokut's homelands were in central California. The people were divided into the Northern Valley Yokut, the Southern Valley Yokut, and the Foothill Yokut.

The Northern Valley Yokut lived along the San Joaquin (san-wah-KEEN) River. Their western boundary was the Diablo Range. The Sierra Nevada was the eastern boundary. Oak trees grew in the wet areas of these lands.

The Southern Valley Yokut lived in the San Joaquin Valley. The land was made up of many rivers, lakes, and wetlands. The lands were home to numerous birds, animals, and plants.

A stream flows through the traditional Yokut homelands.

Sycamore trees, willow, and **tule** (TOO-lee) grew along the riverbanks.

The Foothill Yokut lived in the San Joaquin Valley and the foothills of the Sierra Nevada. The territory was made up of wetlands, grasslands, mountains, and rivers. Oaks and **conifer** trees grew in the mountains.

Yokut Homelands

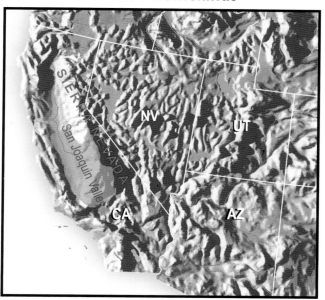

5

Society

The Yokut lived in settlements along large rivers. Many settlements lay scattered throughout Yokut territory. These settlements were divided into clans. Each clan had its own animal **totem**. Some totems were Eagle, Dove, Falcon, Magpie, Bear, Cougar, Blue Jay, and Rattlesnake.

Each settlement had a chief. Most often, chiefs were from the Eagle clan. Chiefs were responsible for welcoming visitors and keeping the peace. They set dates for ceremonies and hunting and gathering trips. Chiefs also helped feed the poor.

Each chief had an assistant. This person was from the Dove clan and acted as a messenger. When on official business, the assistant carried a tall cane with beads attached to it. Each settlement also had a spokesman. This person had Magpie as a totem. A spokesman's job was to speak to the people.

Medicine people were also a part of the settlements. Medicine people had special healing powers. Some performed ceremonies to chase away rattlesnakes or to bring good weather. Bear medicine people were said to be able to turn into bears.

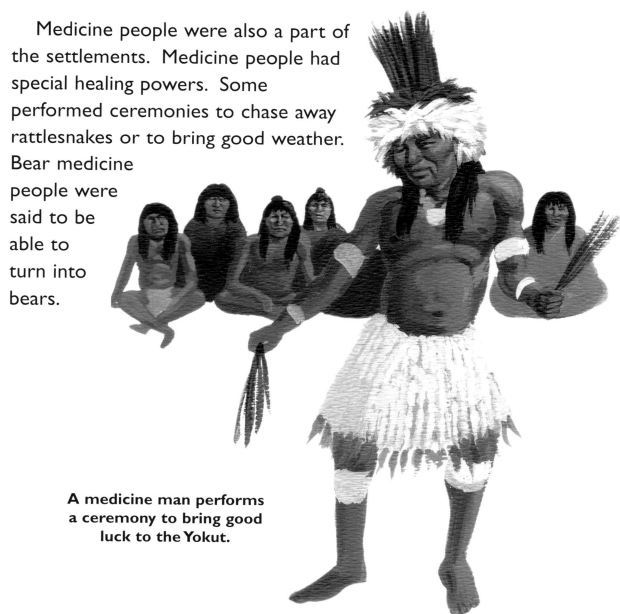

A medicine man performs a ceremony to bring good luck to the Yokut.

7

Food

The Yokut hunted, fished, and gathered food from their lands. Men hunted large animals, such as mule deer and **tule** elks. To do this, they used **sinew**-backed bows and stone-tipped arrows. The Yokut also hunted small animals including ground squirrels, jackrabbits, and quail. They used traps, snares, and nets to hunt these smaller animals.

Men and women caught fish such as trout, perch, and salmon in their homeland's waterways. They fished from tule canoes using spears, nets, and woven basket traps. Divers also scooped up fish in hand nets. To do this, they dragged a net under water as the canoe moved toward shore. The Yokut broiled the fish or dried them in the sun.

The Yokut also gathered freshwater mussels. The people steamed the mussels on beds of tule. On land, women gathered berries, fruits, and wild plants. They also harvested seeds, tule, pine nuts, and acorns.

Acorns were a staple food for the Yokut. They roasted these nuts and ground them into flour. The Yokut carefully prepared the acorns to remove the bitter **tannic** acid. The flour could be made into mush or soup.

The Yokut cooked with hot rocks. They picked up the hot rocks with two green branches. The people used green branches because they are not yet dry, so they don't catch fire easily. They placed the hot rocks inside a basket and cooked acorn soup.

A Yokut woman places hot stones in a basket to cook soup.

9

Homes

The Yokut lived in cone-shaped homes. Each house was built over a pit about 12 inches (30 cm) deep and 15 feet (5 m) across. The frame was a cone made of straight sapling poles. The Yokut set one end of each pole into the ground. Then they tied the other ends together at the top. The people tied three hoops of three different sizes around the poles.

When the frame was finished, the people covered it with **tule** mats. The Foothill Yokut made mats from cedar bark, or used tarweed and pine needles. The Yokut used rope made from milkweed fibers to tie the pieces together.

The Yokut also built *ramadas*. A *ramada* had a roof made of brush but no walls. It provided shade while the Yokut worked. Women often cooked or ground flour under a *ramada*.

Each Yokut village also had a sweathouse. Each sweathouse was about 18 feet (6 m) across and 8 feet (2 m) tall. The building sat over a pit that was a few feet deep. So, the people used a ladder to climb in and out of the sweathouse. Inside, the Yokut poured water over hot rocks, causing steam to fill the sweathouse.

Yokut homes and a *ramada* in the background

Clothing

In the warm California climate, the Yokut did not wear much clothing. What they did wear was usually made from grasses, animal skins, and woven feathers and fur.

Yokut men wore deerskin **breechcloths**. Women wore aprons. The front of an apron was woven grass, while the back was rabbit skin. On cold days, men and women also wore woven rabbit-skin robes.

The Yokut usually went barefoot. However, they sometimes wore moccasins when walking over rocks or rough ground. Moccasins were one piece of leather tied at the ankle.

Sometimes, women wore basket hats. They wore this kind of hat when they went out to gather seeds and acorns. Both men and women wore their hair long. They tied it up with string made from twisted milkweed fibers.

Yokut women also had tattoos. They created the tattoos by rubbing charcoal into small cuts. These tattoos reached from the mouth down to the chest. Men and women pierced their ears and noses, too. They also wore shell bead, wood, and bone necklaces.

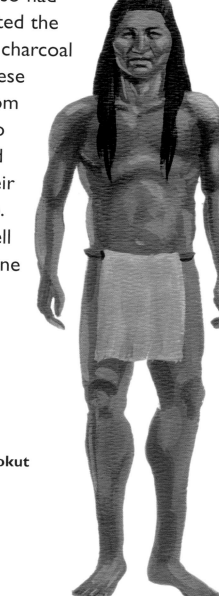

Traditional Yokut clothing

Crafts

The Yokut were excellent basket makers. They wove storage and cooking baskets, as well as their basket hats. The women also made special treasure baskets that often had feathers woven into them.

The Yokut wove these baskets three different ways. They used the coil, twine, or coarse weave methods. Baskets were woven with **tule**, willow, saw grass roots, redbud, and bracken fern.

Hats were made using the coil method. These baskets had beautiful designs. The designs were often **geometric** shapes or human forms.

The twine method was used to make necked water bottles. The weave was so tight that the bottles could hold water. The twine method was also used to make seed beater baskets. The Yokut used seed beaters to knock seeds off grass and into a gathering basket.

A coarse weave was used to make baby cradles. Fish basket traps were also coarsely woven. The traps had one wide end and one narrow end. Fish swam from the wide end into the narrow end and became trapped.

Yokut baskets were useful for other tasks, too. For example, in times of floods, the Yokut put their children inside large baskets. In these baskets, the children could float safely on top of the water.

A Yokut woman weaves decorative baskets.

Family

Extended families lived together in Yokut settlements. The survival of the Yokut depended on each person helping with daily chores.

Yokut families moved with the seasons. As seeds, berries, and acorns became ready to harvest, the people moved closer to the ripe food. Older people often stayed in the main settlement while the younger people traveled.

Yokut women raised the children, gathered, fished, and cooked. They used digging sticks to dig up edible roots and bulbs. Individual women owned sections of land with a lot of seeds or acorns. Each woman decided when her land was to be harvested, and who would do the work.

Men made tools and traded goods with neighboring tribes. Trade was made easier by traveling in long **tule** canoes on the many rivers in Yokut territory. To make one of these canoes, the men gathered **tule** from wetlands. Then, they tied the tule together with rope made of twisted pieces of willow bark.

Yokut men also hunted. They had a special way of capturing deer. A man would sneak into a deer herd wearing a disguise made of a deer head. When he was close enough, he killed a deer with a knife or a bow and arrow.

A Yokut man paddles a tule canoe down the river.

Children

The Yokut cared for their babies by carrying them in cradle baskets. Yokut cradle baskets were willow frames with crossbars. A woven **tule** mattress was attached to the frame.

Yokut children swam and played games. When they were older, they also helped with daily chores. They learned by watching and helping the adults.

Yokut girls learned where to find and gather basket-making materials. The girls then learned to prepare the materials and weave them into baskets. They also learned to make **meal** sifting trays by tying tule together with string.

Boys learned how to make tools. They learned hunting skills by hunting for small animals. They used their own small bows and arrows with sharpened tips.

Yokut children learned to make carrying nets, which were used to haul heavy loads. The children also learned to weave basketry fish traps. They learned about their **culture** from their elders. Children learned their people's dances, songs, and stories.

A Yokut child helps gather tule.

Myths

The Yokut have a story about how they believe the earth was created. A long time ago the earth was flooded. A large eagle with a crow riding on his back flew out of the Sky World. Eagle and Crow flew around looking for land.

Eagle and Crow saw a stump in the water. They rested on the stump. Soon they saw fish swimming around it. Seeing the fish made them hungry. They took turns diving to catch the fish.

Eagle and Crow could not live on the stump forever. They needed mud to make land. Duck swam up to the stump. Then Duck dove, and when he came up he had fish and mud in his bill.

Eagle said to Crow, "If we hunt for fish, maybe Duck will bring up mud." They gave Duck fish in exchange for mud. Soon two big piles of mud formed on the stump. Eagle flew into the sky and noticed that Crow was giving himself more mud than Eagle. Eagle was angry, so they fought.

Eagle decided he would work twice as hard. Soon his pile was bigger than Crow's. As the piles grew, the water level lowered. The sun hardened the mud. This is how Eagle, Crow, and Duck created the earth.

Eagle and Crow make a bargain with Duck.

War

The Yokut were a peaceful and friendly people. The chiefs worked hard to keep the peace. So, the Yokut did not go to war often.

When peace efforts failed, the people sent a messenger to the other tribe. The messenger set the place, date, and time for the war. Then, the speaker announced to the people when they would go to war.

Any brave man could become a war leader. But, this man had to have the Raven as his spiritual helper. The Yokut believed the Raven helped by giving the war leader supernatural powers.

In warfare, the Yokut fought with knives made from bone and antler. They also fought with bows made of cedarwood. They wrapped **sinew** around the bow to make it stronger.

The Yokut shot compound arrows made from reeds and wood. Sinew and asphalt attached a stone arrowhead to the arrow's wooden shaft. The arrows were **fletched** with bird feathers.

A Yokut man readies his
bow and arrow.

Contact with Europeans

In the 1700s, the Yokut had brief encounters with Europeans. The Yokut were friendly to these first Europeans to enter their territory. In 1772, a Spanish soldier and explorer named Pedro Fages led soldiers into the southern part of the San Joaquin Valley. Later, in 1776, Father Francisco Garcés entered Yokut territory.

More Spanish settlers soon arrived. They built **missions** to convert the tribes of the area to Christianity. Some Yokut, such as those living in the foothills, were isolated from the missionaries. But, others were taken from their lands to nearby missions.

At the missions, the missionaries forced the native people to abandon their **cultural** ways. Some native people escaped the missions to live with the Yokut. Soldiers were sent to capture the escaped people.

In the 1800s, more and more settlers took Yokut lands. As their environment changed, some Yokut started raiding the missions and ranches. They took horses and other livestock.

The Yokut did not have **immunity** to European diseases. In the 1830s, many died from a malaria **epidemic**. In 1870, many embraced the Ghost Dance. They believed the Ghost Dance would bring back their dead ancestors and restore their way of life. But, interest in the dance faded a few years later.

A Yokut man meets Father Garcés.

Chief Estanislao

Chief Estanislao was a Northern Valley Yokut. His Yokut name was Cucunuchi. He eventually came to live at a Spanish **mission**. There, he was baptized and given the name Estanislao. He was forced to change his traditional way of life and work for the mission.

The missionaries came to respect Estanislao. They gave him the title of *alcalde*, or "mayor." However, Estanislao soon grew angry with the missionaries. He knew the Yokut and other native people worked hard but were treated poorly. He saw how following new ways was causing them to forget their language and **culture**.

In 1828, Estanislao rebelled and escaped from the mission system. He took a group of his people back to Yokut lands in the San Joaquin Valley. The mission sent soldiers to bring them back.

Chief Estanislao

Estanislao and his group defeated two military expeditions. The third, led by Mexico's Mariano Vallejo, was armed with cannons. Vallejo claimed victory, but he returned without Estanislao or any of his group.

The Yokut Today

Over the years, the Yokut lost many people and almost all of their homelands. As a result, they also lost many of their traditional ways of life. In 1873, the U.S. government moved many Yokut to the **Tule** River Reservation. The Santa Rosa Rancheria was created for the Yokut later, in the mid-1900s.

Today there are about 2,000 Yokut people. They live on three **federally recognized** rancherias and one reservation. They are the Santa Rosa, Picayune, and Table Mountain Rancherias, and the Tule River Reservation. The Tule River Reservation includes people from many Yokut tribes.

Sunset over the Sierra Nevada

A coil-woven Yokut basket

In 1988, the U.S. Congress passed the Indian Gaming Regulatory Act. The act allows tribes such as the Tachi Yokut of Santa Rosa Rancheria to have gaming facilities. The Tachi are using money made from their Palace Indian Gaming Center to restore their language and **cultural** traditions. The money helps pay for education, housing, and other programs.

The Sierra Nevada, on traditional Yokut land

Glossary

breechcloth - a piece of hide or cloth, usually worn by men, that wraps between the legs and ties with a belt around the waist.

conifer - a tree or shrub that bears needles or cones and keeps its needles in the winter.

culture - the customs, arts, or tools of a nation or people at a certain time.

epidemic - the rapid spread of a disease among many people.

federal recognition - the U.S. government's recognition of a tribe as being an independent nation. The tribe is then eligible for special funding and for protection of its reservation lands.

fletch - to put feathers on the end of an arrow.

geometric - made up of straight lines, circles, and other simple shapes.

immunity - protection against disease.

meal - coarsely ground seeds.

mission - a center or headquarters for religious work.

sinew - a band of tough fibers that joins a muscle to another part, such as a bone.

tannic - related to tannin, a bitter-tasting yellow or brown mix of chemicals.

totem - an item that serves as a symbol of a particular family or clan.

tule - a type of reed that grows in wetlands. Tule is native to California.

Web Sites

To learn more about the Yokut, visit ABDO Publishing Company on the World Wide Web at **www.abdopub.com**. Web sites about the Yokut are featured on our Book Links page. These links are routinely monitored and updated to provide the most current information available.

Index